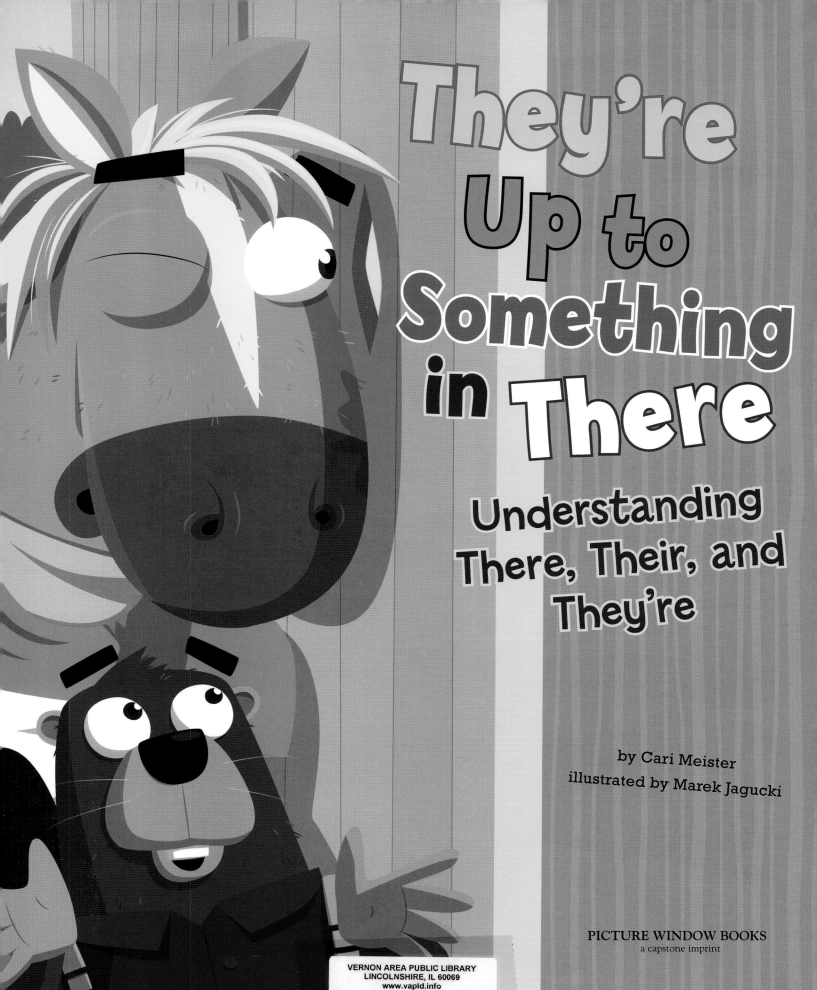

They're Up to Something in There

Understanding There, Their, and They're

by Cari Meister

illustrated by Marek Jagucki

PICTURE WINDOW BOOKS
a capstone imprint

2

Later, in Oscar's workshop ...

15

The next day, at the contest ...

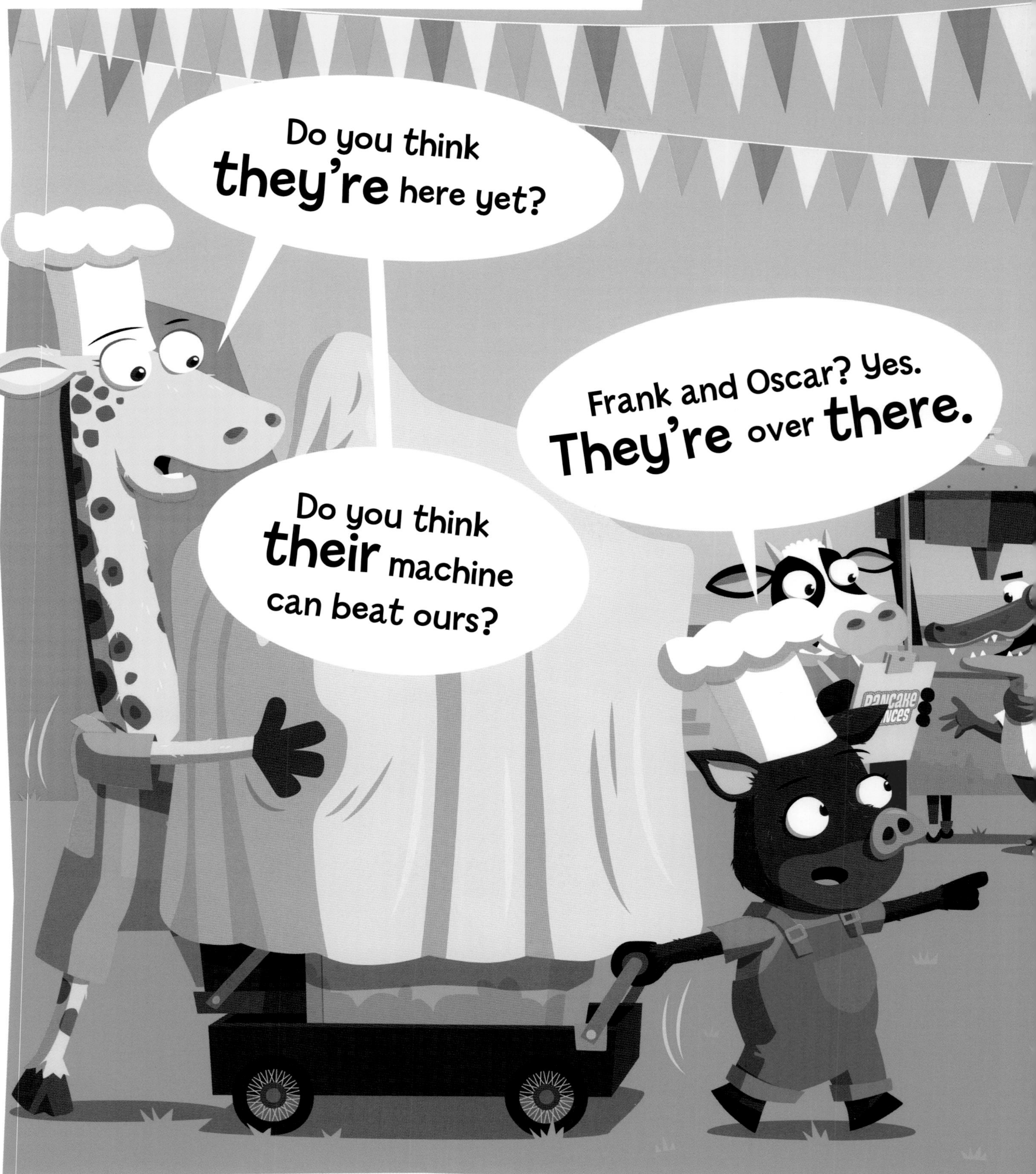

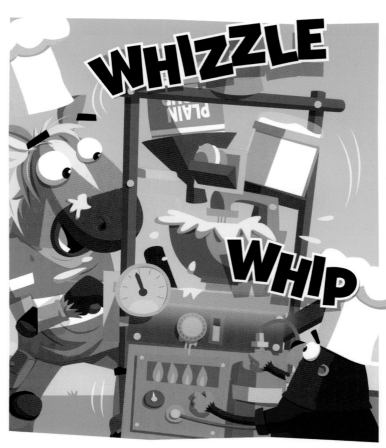

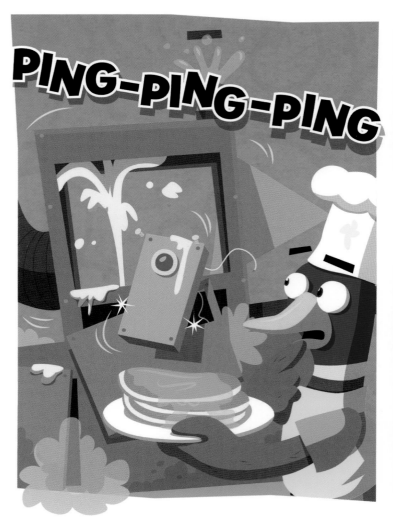

About There, Their, and They're

The words "there," "their," and "they're" are homophones—words that sound the same but are spelled differently and have different meanings. Understanding when to use these three words can be tricky. It is important to use the right one when you are writing. So what exactly is the difference between them?

THERE

The word "there" stands for a place or location. It is similar to the word "here." It may be helpful for you to find the word "here" in the word "there."

There is our summer camp.
Please put the tent up over **there**.

"There" can also stand for an idea.

There are many kinds of pie.
There is only one winner.

THEIR

The word "their" is a possessive word. It shows ownership. "Their" is similar to the words "his," "her," and "our."

Their dog ran after the truck.
It is our turn to go to **their** house.

THEY'RE

The word "they're" actually stands for two words: "they are." It is a contraction. If you are not sure if you should use "they're," you can always say the words "they are" in the sentence to see if it makes sense.

They're going to get ice cream.
They're very happy.

Now you know what THEY'RE up to in THERE. You've seen THEIR machines. THERE isn't much more to say, is THERE?

Read More

Cleary, Brian P. *How Much Can a Bare Bear Bear?: What Are Homonyms and Homophones?* Words Are Categorical. Minneapolis: Millbrook Press, 2005.

Coffelt, Nancy. *Aunt Ant Leaves Through the Leaves: A Story with Homophones and Homonyms.* New York: Holiday House, 2012.

Loewen, Nancy. *If You Were a Homonym or a Homophone.* Word Fun. Minneapolis: Picture Window Books, 2007.

Internet Sites

FactHound offers a safe, fun way to find Internet sites related to this book. All of the sites on FactHound have been researched by our staff.

Here's all you do:

Visit *www.facthound.com*

Type in this code: 9781479569670

Super-cool stuff! Check out projects, games and lots more at **www.capstonekids.com**

Special thanks to our adviser, Terry Flaherty, PhD, Professor of English, Minnesota State University, Mankato, for his expertise.

Editor: Jill Kalz
Designer: Ted Williams
Creative Director: Nathan Gassman
Production Specialist: Katy LaVigne
The illustrations in this book were created digitally.

Picture Window Books are published by Capstone, 1710 Roe Crest Drive, North Mankato, Minnesota 56003
www.capstonepub.com

Library of Congress Cataloging-in-Publication Data
Meister, Cari.
They're up to something in there : understanding there, their, and they're / by Cari Meister.
    pages cm. — (Picture window books. Language on the loose.)
  Includes bibliographical references and index.
  Summary: "Introduces the differences between "there," "their," and "they're" through the telling of an original story"—Provided by publisher.
  ISBN 978-1-4795-6967-0 (library binding)
  ISBN 978-1-4795-6971-7 (paperback)
  ISBN 978-1-4795-6975-5 (eBook PDF)
1. English language—Homonyms—Juvenile literature.
2. English language—Homonyms—Study and teaching (Elementary) I. Title. II. Title: Understanding there, their, and they're.
PE1595.M453 2016
428.1—dc23   2014049208

Look for all the books in the series:

The BIG Problem (and the Squirrel Who Eventually Solved It)
Understanding Adjectives and Adverbs

The Duckster Ducklings Go to Mars
Understanding Capitalization

Frog. Frog? Frog!
Understanding Sentence Types

Monsters Can Mosey
Understanding Shades of Meaning

Sasha Sings
Understanding Parts of a Sentence

They're Up to Something in There
Understanding There, Their, and They're

whatever says mark
Knowing and Using Punctuation

When and Why Did the Horse Fly?
Knowing and Using Question Words

Printed in the United States of America in North Mankato, Minnesota.   042015   008823CGF15